CKD STAGE 3 COOKBOOK FOR

SENIORS

"40 Kidney-friendly Diet for Seniors on

Stage 3"

ALLIE NAGEL

Copyright © 2024 by Allie Nagel

DISCLAIMER

This cookbook is intended to provide general information and recipes.

The recipes provided in this cookbook are not intended to replace or be a substitute for medical advice from a physician.

The reader should consult a healthcare professional for any specific medical advice, diagnosis or treatment.

Any specific dietary advice provided in this cookbook is not intended to replace or be a substitute for medical advice from a physician.

The author is not responsible or liable for any adverse effects experienced by readers of this cookbook as a result of following the recipes or dietary advice provided.

The author makes no representations or warranties of any kind (express or implied) as to the accuracy, completeness, reliability or suitability of the recipes provided in this cookbook.

The author disclaims any and all liability for any damages arising out of the use or misuse of the recipes provided in this cookbook. The reader must also take care to ensure that the recipes provided in this cookbook are prepared and cooked safely.

The recipes provided in this cookbook are for informational purposes only and should not be used as a substitute for professional medical advice, diagnosis or treatment.

TABLE OF CONTENTS

INTRODUCTION 9

CHAPTER 1 11

MANAGING DIABETES WITH CKD 11

DIETARY GUIDELINES FOR SENIORS WITH CKD
.... 13

THE IMPORTANCE OF PORTION CONTROL FOR
KIDNEY HEALTH... 16

CHAPTER 2 19

14-DAY MEAL PLAN 19

CHAPTER 3 23

40 NUTRITIOUS FOR A CKD STAGE 3 DIET FOR
SENIORS RECIPES.. 23

BREAKFAST 23

Scrambled Egg Whites with Lettuce............................ 23

Rice Pudding with Blueberries 24

Apple Cinnamon Rice Cake.. 25

Kidney-Friendly Eggplant Parmesan with No-Sodium
Cottage Cheese... 25

Kidney-Friendly Rice Porridge with Blueberries 27

Kidney-Friendly Egg Salad with Whole White Bread Sandwich 28

Vegetable Omelet 29

Peach Smoothie 30

White Bread French Toast with Applesauce 31

Kidney-Friendly Melon Salad 33

LUNCH 34

Grilled Chicken Salad with Mixed Greens 34

Fresh Tuna Salad on Whole Wheat Bread 35

Pasta with Garlic and Olive Oil 36

Cauliflower Salad with Peas and Carrots 37

Vegetable Soup with Lettuce and Bell Peppers 39

Chicken Caesar Salad 40

Shrimp and Broccoli Stir-Fry 42

Beef Stew with Carrots and Celery 43

Fresh Turkey Burger 44

Baked Cod with Herbs (Kidney-Friendly Version) 46

DINNER 47

Herb Chicken with Zucchini and Bell Peppers............. 47

Baked Tilapia with Steamed Kale............................... 49

Cauliflower Rice Stir-Fry with Mixed Vegetables........ 51

Grilled Turkey Burgers with Lettuce Wraps 53

Vegetable Stew with Carrots, Green Beans, and Celery 54

Grilled Shrimp Salad with Mixed Greens and Vinaigrette
.... 56

Baked Salmon with Dill, served with Asparagus.......... 57

Chicken and Rice Casserole with Peas and Carrots...... 58

Baked Cod with Pepper Seasoning and Sautéed Lettuce
.... 60

Grilled Chicken Caesar Salad (with Low-Sodium
Dressing).. 61

DESSERTS 63

Strawberry Shortcake (Kidney-Friendly Version) 63

Cheesecake Bites with White Flour 64

Roasted Pears (Kidney-Friendly Version).................... 66

White Rice Pudding (Kidney-Friendly Version)........... 67

Baked Apples with Cinnamon (Kidney-Friendly Version) 68

SOUPS AND STEWS 69

Mushroom Cabbage Soup with Skinless Chicken 69

Zucchini and Bell Pepper Soup 71

Vegetable Broth Soup 72

Cabbage and Bell Pepper Stew 73

Cauliflower Soup 74

CONCLUSION 76

INTRODUCTION

Chronic Kidney Disease (CKD) stage 3 marks a moderate decline in kidney function. Seniors like you with CKD stage 3 need a carefully balanced diet to manage the progression of the disease and maintain your overall health.

This stage is characterized by a glomerular filtration rate (GFR) of 30 to 59 ml/min, indicating the kidneys aren't functioning at full capacity.

The dietary focus for seniors in this stage involves controlling certain nutrients to reduce kidney strain while ensuring adequate nutritional intake.

Firstly, protein consumption should be moderated. Excessive protein can increase the burden on kidneys, so a balanced amount is crucial.

High-quality proteins like lean meats, eggs, and fish are recommended, but in controlled portions. However, underconsumption of protein can lead to malnutrition, especially in seniors, so careful monitoring is necessary.

Sodium intake needs to be limited to help control blood pressure, a common issue in CKD patients. Seniors should avoid high-sodium foods and use herbs and spices for flavoring instead of salt. This helps in reducing the risk of fluid retention and hypertension.

Potassium levels must also be managed. While potassium is essential for muscle function, including the heart, impaired kidneys can't filter excess potassium efficiently. This can lead to dangerous levels in the blood. Foods high in potassium, like bananas, oranges, and potatoes, should be consumed in moderation.

Phosphorus is another mineral to watch. Too much phosphorus can weaken bones as kidneys lose their ability to maintain calcium-phosphorus balance. You should limit dairy products and opt for lower-phosphorus alternatives.

Fluid intake may also need adjustment. While staying hydrated is important, too much fluid can lead to swelling and heart issues in CKD patients. The exact fluid needs can vary, so it's essential to follow individualized advice from healthcare providers.

CHAPTER 1

MANAGING DIABETES WITH CKD

Managing diabetes in conjunction with chronic kidney disease (CKD) presents unique challenges, as both conditions require careful dietary and lifestyle considerations to manage effectively. The goal is to control blood sugar levels while protecting kidney function, as diabetes is a leading cause of CKD.

DIET CONSIDERATIONS:

1. **Carbohydrate Management:** Consistent carbohydrate intake at meals is crucial for blood sugar control. Focus on complex carbohydrates with a low glycemic index, such as whole grains, legumes, and vegetables, to prevent spikes in blood sugar.

2. **Protein Intake:** Protein needs may vary. In early stages of CKD, a normal protein diet is often recommended for diabetic patients, but as CKD progresses, a reduction in protein intake may be necessary to lessen kidney strain. High-quality

protein sources like fish, egg whites, and lean poultry are preferred.

3. **Sodium Restriction:** High sodium intake can increase blood pressure, worsening both diabetes and CKD. Limiting processed and canned foods, and seasoning with herbs and spices instead of salt, can help manage blood pressure.

4. **Potassium and Phosphorus Control:** Advanced CKD may require restrictions in potassium and phosphorus. Potassium-rich foods like bananas, oranges, and potatoes, and phosphorus-rich foods like dairy products, nuts, and seeds may need to be limited depending on individual blood levels.

5. **Healthy Fats:** Incorporate heart-healthy fats from sources like olive oil, avocados, and nuts. These can improve cholesterol levels, benefiting both heart health and diabetes management.

LIFESTYLE CONSIDERATIONS:

1. **Regular Monitoring:** Frequent monitoring of blood glucose, kidney function tests, and blood pressure is vital. It helps in adjusting medications and diet as needed.

2. **Physical Activity:** Regular exercise can help control blood sugar and blood pressure, and it promotes overall kidney health. Activities should be chosen based on individual ability and preferences.

3. **Medication Management:** Some diabetes medications need adjustment in CKD, as reduced kidney function can affect drug metabolism and excretion.

4. **Smoking Cessation:** Smoking can accelerate the progression of both diabetes and CKD, so quitting is highly beneficial.

5. **Regular Healthcare Visits:** Regular check-ups with healthcare providers, including a nephrologist, endocrinologist, and dietitian, are essential for managing the complexities of both conditions.

DIETARY GUIDELINES FOR SENIORS WITH CKD

1. **Control Protein Intake:** Depending on the stage of CKD, protein intake may need to be limited to reduce kidney strain. High-quality proteins are preferred.

2. **Limit Sodium:** High sodium intake can increase blood pressure and worsen kidney damage. Seniors should avoid salty foods and season meals with herbs and spices instead of salt.

3. **Potassium Management:** Depending on kidney function, potassium levels might need to be monitored. Some may need to limit high-potassium foods like bananas and potatoes.

4. **Phosphorus Control:** Excessive phosphorus can affect bone health in CKD patients. Foods high in phosphorus, like dairy products and nuts, might need to be limited.

5. **Adequate Caloric Intake:** Seniors should ensure they are consuming enough calories to maintain their weight and energy levels.

6. **Fluid Intake:** Fluid needs can vary. Some individuals with CKD need to restrict fluids to prevent fluid overload and swelling.

7. **Balanced Diet:** A diet rich in fruits, vegetables, whole grains, and lean proteins provides essential nutrients without overburdening the kidneys.

8. **Limit Alcohol:** Alcohol can affect blood pressure, kidney function, and medications.

9. **Healthy Fats:** Incorporating healthy fats like monounsaturated and polyunsaturated fats can support heart health.

10. **Control Blood Sugar:** For diabetics, managing blood sugar levels is crucial in slowing the progression of CKD.

11. **Fiber Intake:** Fiber is important for digestive health and can help control blood sugar and cholesterol levels.

12. **Avoid Smoking:** Smoking can worsen kidney damage and should be avoided.

13. **Regular Monitoring:** Regular monitoring of kidney function, blood pressure, and blood sugar levels can guide dietary adjustments.

14. **Stay Hydrated:** Proper hydration is important, but fluid intake should be balanced with kidney function.

15. **Consult Healthcare Professionals:** Regular consultations with healthcare providers, including dietitians specialized in kidney health, are essential for personalized dietary advice.

THE IMPORTANCE OF PORTION CONTROL FOR KIDNEY HEALTH

1. **Nutrient Balance:** Kidneys are responsible for filtering excess nutrients from the blood. By controlling portions, one can avoid overconsumption of nutrients like sodium, potassium, phosphorus, and protein, which in excess can be hard on the kidneys.

2. **Managing Blood Pressure:** Overeating, particularly high-sodium foods, can lead to high blood pressure, a major risk factor for kidney damage. Portion control helps in managing blood pressure levels.

3. **Regulating Blood Sugar:** For diabetics or those at risk, portion control is essential in managing blood sugar levels. Uncontrolled diabetes is a leading cause of kidney disease.

4. **Weight Management:** Obesity is a risk factor for chronic kidney disease. Controlling portions helps in maintaining a healthy weight, thereby reducing the strain on the kidneys.

5. **Reducing Kidney Strain:** Overeating makes the kidneys work harder to filter and eliminate waste.

Controlled portions lessen this burden, helping to preserve kidney function.

6. **Avoiding Toxic Build-up:** When kidneys are not functioning optimally, certain substances in food can build up to toxic levels in the blood. Portion control can prevent this.

7. **Fluid Balance:** Especially in later stages of kidney disease, managing fluid intake is crucial to prevent fluid overload, which can lead to swelling and heart problems.

8. **Preventing Malnutrition:** Portion control also means ensuring adequate intake of essential nutrients. It's about eating the right amount – not too little, not too much.

9. **Adherence to Dietary Restrictions:** For those with dietary limitations due to kidney disease, portion control helps in adhering to these restrictions more effectively.

10. **Improving Overall Health:** Good portion control is part of a healthy lifestyle, which benefits overall health and can indirectly support kidney function.

CHAPTER 2

14-DAY MEAL PLAN

DAY 1

Breakfast: Scrambled Egg Whites with Lettuce

Lunch: Grilled Chicken Salad with Mixed Greens

Dinner: Herb Chicken with Zucchini and Bell Peppers

DAY 2

Breakfast: Rice Pudding with Blueberries

Lunch: Fresh Tuna Salad on Whole Wheat Bread

Dinner: Baked Tilapia with Steamed Kale

DAY 3

Breakfast: Apple Cinnamon Rice Cake

Lunch: Pasta with Garlic and Olive Oil

Dinner: Cauliflower Rice Stir-Fry with Mixed Vegetables

DAY 4

Breakfast: Kidney-Friendly Rice Porridge with Berries

Lunch: Cauliflower Salad with Peas and Carrots

Dinner: Grilled Turkey Burgers with Lettuce Wraps

DAY 5

Breakfast: Kidney-Friendly Eggplant Parmesan with No-Sodium Cottage Cheese

Lunch: Vegetable Soup with Kale and Bell Peppers

Dinner: Vegetable Stew with Carrots, Green Beans, and Celery

DAY 6

Breakfast: Kidney-Friendly Egg Salad with Whole Grain Bread Sandwich

Lunch: Chicken Caesar Salad

Dinner: Grilled Shrimp Salad with Mixed Greens and Vinaigrette

DAY 7

Breakfast: Vegetable Omelet

Lunch: Shrimp and Broccoli Stir-Fry

Dinner: Baked Salmon with Dill and Lemon, served with Asparagus

DAY 8

Breakfast: Peach Smoothie

Lunch: Beef Stew with Carrots and Celery

Dinner: Chicken and Rice Casserole with Peas and Carrots

DAY 9

Breakfast: White Bread French Toast with Applesauce

Lunch: Fresh Turkey Burger

Dinner: Baked Cod with Lemon Pepper Seasoning and Sautéed Kale

DAY 10

Breakfast: Kidney-Friendly Melon Salad

Lunch: Baked Cod with Herbs (Kidney-Friendly Version)

Dinner: Grilled Chicken Caesar Salad

DAY 11

Breakfast: Scrambled Egg Whites with Lettuce

Lunch: Grilled Chicken Salad with Mixed Greens

Dinner: Herb Chicken with Zucchini and Bell Peppers

DAY 12

Breakfast: Rice Pudding with Blueberries

Lunch: Fresh Tuna Salad on Whole Wheat Bread

Dinner: Baked Tilapia with Steamed Kale

DAY 13

Breakfast: Apple Cinnamon Rice Cake

Lunch: Pasta with Garlic and Olive Oil

Dinner: Cauliflower Rice Stir-Fry with Mixed Vegetables

DAY 14

Breakfast: Kidney-Friendly Eggplant Parmesan with No-Sodium Cottage Cheese

Lunch: Cauliflower Salad with Peas and Carrots

Dinner: Grilled Turkey Burgers with Lettuce Wraps

CHAPTER 3

40 NUTRITIOUS FOR A CKD STAGE 3 DIET FOR SENIORS RECIPES

BREAKFAST

Scrambled Egg Whites with Lettuce

Preparation Time: 5 Minutes

Serves: 1

Calories: 120

Ingredients:

4 egg whites

1 cup fresh lettuce, chopped

Pepper to taste

Method of Preparation:

1. In a bowl, whisk the egg whites until frothy.
2. Heat a non-stick pan over medium heat and add the chopped lettuce.

3. Once the lettuce is wilted, pour the egg whites over it.
4. Stir continuously until the eggs are cooked through.
5. Season with Pepper to taste.

Rice Pudding with Blueberries

Preparation Time: 10 Minutes

Serves: 1

Calories: 200

Ingredients:

1/2 cup White Rice

1 cup water or low-phosphorus milk

1/4 cup fresh blueberries

1 tablespoon honey (optional)

Method of Preparation:

1. Cook white rice according to package instructions using water or low-phosphorus milk.
2. Once cooked, top with fresh blueberries and milk.
3. Drizzle with honey if desired.

Apple Cinnamon Rice Cake

Preparation Time: 20 Minutes

Serves: 1

Calories: 70

Ingredients:

1 rice cake (choose a low-sodium option)

1/2 medium apple, thinly sliced

1/2 teaspoon cinnamon

Method of Preparation:

1. Place thinly sliced apples on top of the rice cake.
2. Sprinkle with cinnamon.

Kidney-Friendly Eggplant Parmesan with No-Sodium Cottage Cheese

Preparation Time: 30 Minutes

Serves: 4

Calories: 250

Ingredients:

1 large eggplant, sliced

1 cup no-sodium added cottage cheese

1 cup low-sodium tomato sauce

1 cup shredded low-fat mozzarella cheese

1/2 cup grated Parmesan cheese

1 teaspoon dried oregano

1 teaspoon dried basil

1/2 teaspoon garlic powder

substitute to taste

Olive oil for baking

Method of Preparation:

1. Preheat oven to 375°F (190°C).
2. eggplant slices and let them sit for 30 minutes to draw out excess moisture. Rinse and pat dry.
3. In a bowl, mix cottage cheese with oregano, basil, and garlic powder.

4. In a baking dish, layer eggplant slices, followed by cottage cheese mixture, tomato sauce, and mozzarella.
5. Repeat layers and top with Parmesan cheese.
6. Bake for 30-35 minutes until bubbly and golden.
7. Let it rest for 10 minutes before Serves.

Kidney-Friendly Rice Porridge with Blueberries

Preparation Time: 30 Minutes

Serves: 4

Calories: 200

Ingredients:

1 cup white rice

4 cups water

1 cup blueberries

2 tablespoons honey or a sugar substitute

1/2 teaspoon cinnamon

1/4 cup chopped almonds (optional)

Method of Preparation:

1. Rinse rice and cook with water until soft and porridge-like.
2. Stir in honey or sugar substitute and cinnamon.
3. Top with mixed berries and almonds if desired.

Kidney-Friendly Egg Salad with Whole White Bread Sandwich

Preparation Time: 20 Minutes

Serves: 4

Calories: 300

Ingredients:

6 hard-boiled eggs, chopped

1/2 cup low-sodium mayonnaise

1 tablespoon Dijon mustard

1/4 cup chopped green onions

Pepper to taste

Whole White bread slices

Method of Preparation:

1. In a bowl, mix chopped eggs, mayonnaise, Dijon mustard, and green onions.
2. Season with pepper to taste.
3. Spread the egg salad on whole white bread slices to make sandwiches.

Vegetable Omelet

Preparation Time: 5 Minutes

Serves: 1

Calories: 250

Ingredients:

2 large eggs

1/4 cup diced bell peppers (any color)

1/4 cup chopped lettuce

1 tablespoon chopped chives

1 teaspoon olive oil

Pepper to taste

2 tablespoons low-phosphorus cheese (optional)

Method of Preparation:

1. In a bowl, whisk the eggs until well beaten.
2. Heat olive oil in a non-stick pan over medium heat.
3. Add bell peppers, and lettuce to the pan, sauté for 2-3 minutes until vegetables are slightly softened.
4. Pour beaten eggs over the vegetables in the pan.
5. Sprinkle chives, and pepper over the eggs.
6. Cook until the edges are set, then gently lift the edges and tilt the pan to let the uncooked eggs flow to the edges.
7. Optional: Add low-phosphorus cheese on one half of the omelet.
8. Once the eggs are mostly set, fold the omelet in half and cook for an additional minute.
9. Slide onto a plate, and serve hot.

Peach Smoothie

Preparation Time: 5 Minutes

Serves: 1

Calories: 180

Ingredients:

1 cup frozen peaches (unsweetened)

1/2 cup low-potassium yogurt

1/2 cup almond milk (or other low-potassium milk)

1 tablespoon honey (optional)

1/2 teaspoon vanilla extract

Ice cubes (optional)

Method of Preparation:

1. In a blender, combine frozen peaches, low-potassium yogurt, almond milk, honey (if using), and vanilla extract.
2. Blend until smooth and creamy.
3. Add ice cubes if a colder consistency is desired and blend again.
4. Taste and adjust sweetness if needed.

White Bread French Toast with Applesauce

Preparation Time: 15 Minutes

Serves: 2

Calories: 250

Ingredients:

4 slices white bread (low-sodium)

2 large eggs

1 cup unsweetened applesauce

1 teaspoon cinnamon

1/2 teaspoon vanilla extract

Cooking spray

Method of Preparation:

1. In a bowl, whisk together eggs, cinnamon, and vanilla extract.
2. Dip each slice of bread into the egg mixture, ensuring both sides are coated.
3. Heat a non-stick pan over medium heat and lightly coat it with cooking spray.
4. Cook each bread slice until golden brown on both sides.
5. Serve with a side of unsweetened applesauce.

Kidney-Friendly Melon Salad

Preparation Time:

Serves: 4

Calories: 70

Ingredients:

2 cups watermelon, cubed

2 cups cantaloupe, cubed

2 cups honeydew melon, cubed

1 tablespoon fresh mint, chopped

1 tablespoon lime juice

Method of Preparation:

1. In a large bowl, combine watermelon, cantaloupe, and honeydew melon.
2. Sprinkle fresh mint over the melon mixture.
3. Drizzle lime juice over the salad and gently toss to combine.

LUNCH

Grilled Chicken Salad with Mixed Greens

Preparation Time: 30 Minutes

Serves: 4

Calories: 300

Ingredients:

Boneless, skinless chicken breasts

Mixed salad greens (e.g., lettuce, arugula, and romaine)

Cherry tomatoes, halved

Cucumber, sliced

Red bell pepper, diced

Olive oil

Balsamic vinegar

Pepper to taste

Method of Preparation:

1. Season chicken breasts with pepper.
2. Grill chicken until fully cooked, then slice.
3. In a large bowl, combine mixed greens, cucumber, and red bell pepper.
4. Top the salad with grilled chicken slices.
5. Drizzle olive oil and balsamic vinegar over the salad.
6. Toss gently and serve.

Fresh Tuna Salad on Whole Wheat Bread

Preparation Time: 20 Minutes

Serves: 2

Calories: 350

Ingredients:

Fresh tuna, cooked and flaked

Whole wheat bread slices

Celery, finely chopped

Red onion, finely chopped

Greek yogurt (as a mayo substitute)

Dijon mustard

Lemon juice

Pepper to taste

Method of Preparation:

1. In a bowl, mix flaked tuna, celery, red onion, Greek yogurt, Dijon mustard, and lemon juice.
2. Season with pepper.
3. Toast whole wheat bread slices.
4. Spread tuna salad on the bread slices to make sandwiches.

Pasta with Garlic and Olive Oil

Preparation Time: 30 Minutes

Serves: 4

Calories: 250

Ingredients:

Whole-grain pasta

Olive oil

Garlic cloves, minced

Bell peppers

Lettuce leaves

Parmesan cheese (optional)

Pepper to taste

Method of Preparation:

1. Cook whole-grain pasta according to package instructions.
2. In a pan, sauté minced garlic in olive oil until golden.
3. Add Bell pepper and lettuce, sauté until wilted.
4. Toss the cooked pasta into the pan, mixing well.
5. Season with pepper.
6. Optional: Top with grated Parmesan cheese.

Cauliflower Salad with Peas and Carrots

Preparation Time: 2- Minutes

Serves: 4

Calories: 150

Ingredients:

1 medium-sized cauliflower, chopped into small florets

1 cup frozen peas

1 cup diced carrots

2 tablespoons olive oil

2 tablespoons white wine vinegar

1 teaspoon Dijon mustard

1 teaspoon dried oregano

Pepper to taste

1/4 cup chopped fresh parsley (optional)

Method of Preparation:

1. Steam cauliflower until tender, then cool.
2. Boil peas and carrots until just cooked, then cool.
3. In a large bowl, combine cauliflower, peas, and carrots.
4. In a small bowl, whisk together olive oil, white wine vinegar, Dijon mustard, oregano, and pepper.

5. Pour dressing over vegetables and toss until well-coated.

6. Garnish with fresh parsley if desired.

Vegetable Soup with Lettuce and Bell Peppers

Preparation Time: 30 Minutes

Serves: 6

Calories: 120

Ingredients:

1 tablespoon olive oil

1 cup diced onion

2 cloves garlic, minced

4 cups low-sodium vegetable broth

1 cup chopped lettuce; stems removed

1 cup diced bell peppers (any color)

1 cup diced zucchini

1 can (15 oz) low-sodium diced tomatoes

1 teaspoon dried thyme

Pepper to taste

Fresh lemon juice for Serves

Method of Preparation:

1. In a large pot, heat olive oil and sauté onion and garlic until softened.
2. Add vegetable broth, lettuce, bell peppers, zucchini, diced bell peppers, thyme, salt, and pepper.
3. Simmer for 15-20 minutes until vegetables are tender.
4. Adjust seasoning if necessary and serve with a squeeze of fresh lemon juice.

Chicken Caesar Salad

Preparation Time: 10 Minutes

Serves: 2

Calories: 300

Ingredients:

2 boneless, skinless chicken breasts

1 head romaine lettuce, washed and chopped

Bell peppers

1/4 cup grated Parmesan cheese

1/2 cup croutons (optional)

Caesar dressing (see kidney-friendly alternative below)

Kidney-Friendly Caesar Dressing:

1/4 cup plain Greek yogurt

1 tablespoon lemon juice

1 tablespoon olive oil

1 clove garlic, minced

1 teaspoon Dijon mustard

Pepper to taste

Method of Preparation:

1. Grill or bake chicken breasts until fully cooked, then slice.
2. In a large bowl, combine romaine lettuce, bell peppers, Parmesan cheese, and croutons.

3. In a separate bowl, whisk together the ingredients for the kidney-friendly Caesar dressing.

4. Toss the salad with the dressing and top with sliced grilled chicken.

Shrimp and Broccoli Stir-Fry

Preparation Time: 20 Minutes

Serves: 4

Calories: 350

Ingredients:

1 lb. shrimp, peeled and deveined

4 cups broccoli florets

2 tbsp low-sodium soy sauce

1 tbsp olive oil

2 cloves garlic, minced

1 tsp ginger, grated

1 tbsp rice vinegar

1 tsp sesame oil

2 cups brown rice, cooked (for Serves)

Method of Preparation:

1. In a large skillet, heat olive oil over medium heat.
2. Add garlic and ginger, sauté until fragrant.
3. Add shrimp to the skillet, cook until they turn pink and opaque.
4. Add broccoli, soy sauce, rice vinegar, and sesame oil. Stir-fry until broccoli is tender-crisp.
5. Serve over cooked brown rice.

Beef Stew with Carrots and Celery

Preparation Time: 30 Minutes

Serves: 6

Calories: 300

Ingredients:

1.5 lb. lean beef stew meat, cubed

4 cups low-sodium beef broth

4 carrots, peeled and sliced

4 celery stalks, sliced

1 onion, chopped

2 cloves garlic, minced

Bell pepper

1 tsp thyme

1 bay leaf

Pepper to taste

Method of Preparation:

1. In a large pot, brown the beef cubes over medium heat.
2. Add onions and garlic, sauté until softened.
3. Stir in bell pepper, thyme, and season with pepper.
4. Pour in beef broth, add carrots, celery, and bay leaf. Bring to a simmer.
5. Reduce heat, cover, and let it simmer until the beef is tender and vegetables are cooked.

Fresh Turkey Burger

Preparation Time: 30 Minutes

Serves: 2

Calories: 250-300

Ingredients:

1 lb. ground turkey (lean)

1/4 cup finely chopped onion

1/4 cup finely chopped bell pepper

1 clove garlic, minced

1/4 cup breadcrumbs (use kidney-friendly option)

1 egg

1 teaspoon Worcestershire sauce

Pepper to taste

Whole wheat burger buns

Lettuce, tomato, and other kidney-friendly toppings

Method of Preparation:

1. In a bowl, combine ground turkey, chopped onion, bell pepper, garlic, breadcrumbs, egg, Worcestershire sauce and pepper.
2. Mix well and form the mixture into burger patties.

3. Grill or cook the patties on a stovetop until fully cooked.

4. Toast the whole wheat buns and assemble burgers with kidney-friendly toppings.

Baked Cod with Herbs (Kidney-Friendly Version)

Preparation Time: 30 minutes

Serves: 4

Calories: 200-250

Ingredients:

4 cod fillets (6 ounces each)

2 tablespoons olive oil

1 teaspoon dried thyme (low in potassium)

1 teaspoon dried rosemary

1/2 teaspoon garlic powder

1/2 teaspoon onion powder

Black pepper to taste

Lemon wedges for serving

Method of Preparation:

1. Preheat your oven to 400°F (200°C).
2. Rinse the cod fillets and pat them dry with paper towels.
3. In a small bowl, mix together the olive oil, thyme, rosemary, garlic powder, onion powder, and black pepper.
4. Place the cod fillets in a baking dish.
5. Brush the herb mixture over the cod fillets, ensuring they are well coated.
6. Bake in the preheated oven for about 20 minutes or until the cod flakes easily with a fork.
7. Serve the baked cod with fresh lemon wedges.

DINNER

Herb Chicken with Zucchini and Bell Peppers

Preparation Time: 30 Minutes

Serves: 4

Calories: 300

Ingredients:

4 boneless, skinless chicken breasts

2 medium-sized zucchinis, sliced

2 bell peppers (any color), sliced

2 tablespoons olive oil

2 cloves garlic, minced

1 teaspoon dried thyme

1 teaspoon dried rosemary

1 teaspoon dried oregano

Pepper to taste

Method of Preparation:

1. Preheat the oven to 375°F (190°C).
2. Season the chicken breasts with pepper, and half of the dried herbs.
3. In a large ovenproof skillet, heat olive oil over medium-high heat. Add chicken breasts and sear for 2-3 minutes on each side until golden brown.

4. Remove the chicken from the skillet and set aside.

5. In the same skillet, add more oil if needed. Sauté garlic, zucchini, and bell peppers until slightly tender.

6. Stir in the remaining dried herbs, lemon zest, and lemon juice.

7. Place the seared chicken breasts back into the skillet, arranging them among the vegetables.

8. Transfer the skillet to the preheated oven and bake for 20-25 minutes or until the chicken is cooked through.

9. Serve hot, garnished with additional lemon slices if desired.

Baked Tilapia with Steamed Kale

Preparation Time: 30 Minutes

Serves: 4

Calories: 200-250

Ingredients:

4 tilapia fillets

1 bunch of kale, stems removed and leaves chopped

2 tablespoons olive oil

1 lemon, sliced

2 cloves garlic, minced

1 teaspoon dried oregano

Pepper to taste

Kidney-friendly alternatives:

Limit and opt for herbs and spices for flavor.

Use olive oil in moderation.

Method of Preparation:

1. Preheat the oven to 400°F (200°C).
2. Place tilapia fillets on a baking sheet lined with parchment paper.
3. Drizzle olive oil over the tilapia, then sprinkle with minced garlic, dried oregano and pepper.
4. Arrange lemon slices on top of the fillets.
5. Bake in the preheated oven for 15-20 minutes or until the tilapia is cooked through and flakes easily with a fork.

6. While the tilapia is baking, steam the chopped kale until tender, about 5-7 minutes.

7. Serve the baked tilapia over a bed of steamed kale.

Cauliflower Rice Stir-Fry with Mixed Vegetables

Preparation Time: 20 Minutes

Serves: 4

Calories: 150-200

Ingredients:

1 medium-sized cauliflower, grated or processed into rice-like texture

1 cup broccoli florets

1 cup sliced bell peppers (choose low-potassium colors like red or yellow)

1 cup sliced zucchini

1 cup snap peas, ends trimmed

1 medium carrot, julienned

2 cloves garlic, minced

2 tablespoons low-sodium soy sauce

1 tablespoon olive oil

1 teaspoon ginger, grated

1 tablespoon rice vinegar

1 tablespoon sesame oil (use sparingly)

Freshly ground black pepper to taste

Method of Preparation:

1. Heat olive oil in a large skillet or wok over medium heat.
2. Add minced garlic and grated ginger, sauté for 1-2 minutes until fragrant.
3. Add broccoli, bell peppers, zucchini, snap peas, and carrots to the skillet. Stir-fry for 5-7 minutes until vegetables are tender but still crisp.
4. Push vegetables to one side of the skillet, add cauliflower rice to the empty side. Stir-fry cauliflower for 3-4 minutes until it's cooked but not mushy.

5. Combine cauliflower rice with the mixed vegetables in the skillet.

6. In a small bowl, mix soy sauce, rice vinegar, sesame oil, and black pepper. Pour the sauce over the stir-fry and toss to combine.

7. Cook for an additional 2-3 minutes, ensuring everything is well-coated and heated through.

8. Adjust seasoning if necessary and serve immediately.

Grilled Turkey Burgers with Lettuce Wraps

Preparation Time: 30 Minutes

Serves:

Calories: 250

Ingredients:

1 lb. ground turkey

1/4 cup finely chopped onions

1/4 cup finely chopped bell peppers

1 teaspoon garlic powder

Pepper to taste

Iceberg lettuce leaves for wraps

Optional toppings: tomato slices, cucumber, and low-sodium condiments

Method of Preparation:

1. In a bowl, mix ground turkey, chopped onions, chopped bell peppers, garlic powder, and pepper.
2. Form the mixture into burger patties.
3. Preheat the grill and cook the turkey burgers until fully cooked.
4. Use iceberg lettuce leaves as wraps and place the cooked burger inside.
5. Add your choice of kidney-friendly toppings.

Vegetable Stew with Carrots, Green Beans, and Celery

Preparation Time: 20 Minutes

Serves: 1

Calories: 120

Ingredients:

2 cups carrots, sliced

2 cups green beans, cut into bite-sized pieces

1 cup celery, chopped

1 onion, diced

2 cloves garlic, minced

4 cups low-sodium vegetable broth

1 teaspoon dried thyme

Pepper to taste

Method of Preparation:

1. In a large pot, sauté onions and garlic until softened.
2. Add carrots, green beans, and celery to the pot.
3. Pour in the vegetable broth and add thyme and pepper.
4. Simmer until the vegetables are tender.
5. Adjust seasoning if necessary.

Grilled Shrimp Salad with Mixed Greens and Vinaigrette

Preparation Time: 15 Minutes

Serves: 2

Calories: 150

Ingredients:

1 lb. shrimp, peeled and deveined

Mixed salad greens

Bell pepper

1 cucumber, sliced

Vinaigrette dressing (olive oil, balsamic vinegar, Dijon mustard)

Lemon wedges for garnish

Method of Preparation:

1. Season shrimp with pepper, then grill until fully cooked.

2. In a large bowl, mix mixed greens, bell pepper, and cucumber slices.

3. Top the salad with grilled shrimp.

4. Drizzle with kidney-friendly vinaigrette dressing.

5. Garnish with lemon wedges.

Baked Salmon with Dill, served with Asparagus

Preparation Time:

Serves: 4

Calories: 300-350

Ingredients:

4 salmon fillets

1 tablespoon olive oil

2 tablespoons fresh dill, chopped

pepper, to taste

1 bunch of asparagus, trimmed

Method of Preparation:

1. Preheat the oven to 400°F (200°C).
2. Place the salmon fillets on a baking sheet lined with parchment paper.
3. Drizzle olive oil over the salmon and season with salt, pepper, and chopped dill.
4. Bake in the preheated oven for 15-20 minutes or until the salmon is cooked through and easily flakes with a fork.
5. While the salmon is baking, toss the trimmed asparagus with olive oil, and pepper.
6. Add the asparagus to the baking sheet during the last 10 minutes of the salmon's cooking time, or until the asparagus is tender-crisp.
7. Serve the baked salmon with roasted asparagus.

Chicken and Rice Casserole with Peas and Carrots

Preparation Time: 1 hour

Serves: 4

Calories: 350

Ingredients:

4 boneless, skinless chicken breasts (cut into small pieces)

1 cup white rice (unenriched)

1 cup low-sodium chicken broth

1/2 cup fresh peas

1/2 cup chopped carrots

1/4 cup diced onion

1 tbsp olive oil

1/2 tsp garlic powder

1/2 tsp black pepper

1/4 tsp dried thyme

Method of Preparation:

1. Preheat oven to 350°F (175°C).
2. In a skillet, heat olive oil over medium heat and cook onions until translucent.
3. Add chicken pieces, garlic powder, black pepper, and thyme. Cook until chicken is lightly browned.

4. In a casserole dish, mix the uncooked rice, low-sodium chicken broth, peas, and carrots.

5. Add the cooked chicken and onions to the casserole dish and stir.

6. Cover with foil and bake for 45 minutes, or until rice is tender.

7. Let it cool for a few minutes before serving.

Baked Cod with Pepper Seasoning and Sautéed Lettuce

Preparation Time: 30 minutes

Serves: 4

Calories: 200

Ingredients:

4 cod fillets

1 tsp black pepper

1/2 tsp garlic powder

4 cups chopped lettuce

1 tbsp olive oil

1/4 tsp substitute

Method of Preparation:

1. Preheat oven to 400°F (200°C).
2. Place cod fillets in a baking dish.
3. Mix black pepper, and garlic powder.
4. Brush over cod.
5. Bake for 20-25 minutes or until fish flakes easily with a fork.
6. In a pan, heat olive oil and sauté lettuce until wilted. Season with a substitute.
7. Serve the baked cod with sautéed kale on the side.

Grilled Chicken Caesar Salad (with Low-Sodium Dressing)

Preparation Time: 20 minutes

Serves: 4

Calories: 300

Ingredients:

4 boneless, skinless chicken breasts

8 cups chopped Romaine lettuce

1/2 cup shredded Parmesan cheese

1 cup croutons (low-sodium)

For Dressing: 1/2 cup low-fat mayonnaise, 1 tsp Dijon mustard, 1 tsp Worcestershire sauce (low-sodium), 1/2 tsp garlic powder, 1/2 tsp black pepper

Method of Preparation:

1. Grill chicken breasts until fully cooked and slice them.
2. In a large bowl, toss the Romaine lettuce, Parmesan cheese, and croutons.
3. In a small bowl, whisk together all dressing ingredients.
4. Adjust seasoning to taste.
5. Drizzle the dressing over the salad and add the grilled chicken slices.
6. Toss everything together and serve immediately.

DESSERTS

Strawberry Shortcake (Kidney-Friendly Version)

Preparation Time: 30 minutes

Serves: 6

Calories: 200-250

Ingredients:

2 cups low-protein flour (replaces regular flour to reduce protein intake)

1/2 cup unsalted butter (avoid salted butter to control sodium levels)

1/4 cup sugar (use less if blood sugar control is needed)

1/2 cup milk substitute (almond, rice, or soy milk)

2 tsp baking powder (aluminum-free)

1 tsp vanilla extract

2 cups fresh blueberries, sliced

1/4 cup whipped topping (choose a low-sodium, low-phosphate brand)

Method of Preparation:

1. Preheat the oven to 350°F (175°C).
2. In a bowl, combine the low-protein flour, baking powder, and sugar.
3. Add unsalted butter and mix until the mixture resembles coarse crumbs.
4. Stir in milk substitute and vanilla extract to form a dough.
5. Place dough on a floured surface and roll out to 1/2-inch thickness.
6. Cut into circles using a biscuit cutter.
7. Place on a baking sheet and bake for 15-20 minutes until golden brown.
8. Allow to cool, then split each shortcake and fill with blueberries and a dollop of whipped topping.

Cheesecake Bites with White Flour

Preparation Time: 1 hour (includes chilling time)

Serves: 12 bites

Calories: 150-200

Ingredients:

1 cup low-protein flour

1/4 cup coconut oil (instead of butter)

1/4 cup maple syrup (a natural sweetener)

1 cup-soaked cashews (soak overnight in water)

1/2 tsp vanilla extract

1/4 cup almond milk

Fresh berries for topping

Method of Preparation:

1. Preheat oven to 350°F (175°C).
2. Mix low-protein flour, coconut oil, and a tablespoon of maple syrup to form the crust.
3. Press into the bottom of a lined muffin tin.
4. Bake for 10-15 minutes until slightly golden. Let it cool.
5. Blend-soaked cashews, remaining maple syrup, vanilla extract, and almond milk until smooth.

6. Pour the mixture over the cooled crusts and refrigerate for at least 2 hours.

7. Top with fresh berries before serving.

Roasted Pears (Kidney-Friendly Version)

Preparation Time: 40 minutes

Serves: 4

Calories: 100-150

Ingredients:

4 ripe pears, halved and cored

2 tbsp honey (or less, depending on sweetness preference)

1/2 tsp ground cinnamon

1/4 tsp ground nutmeg (optional)

Fresh mint for garnish (optional)

Method of Preparation:

1. Preheat the oven to 375°F (190°C).

2. Arrange pear halves on a baking sheet.

3. Drizzle with honey and sprinkle with cinnamon and nutmeg.
4. Roast in the oven for 25-30 minutes until pears are tender.
5. Garnish with fresh mint leaves before serving (optional).

White Rice Pudding (Kidney-Friendly Version)

Preparation Time: 45 minutes

Serves: 6

Calories: 200-250

Ingredients:

1 cup white rice (use short-grain rice for creaminess)

4 cups almond milk (or another kidney-friendly milk substitute)

1/3 cup sugar (adjust according to dietary needs)

1 tsp vanilla extract

Cinnamon for garnish

Method of Preparation:

1. In a large saucepan, combine rice and 2 cups of almond milk.
2. Bring to a boil.
3. Reduce heat to low and simmer, stirring occasionally, until the milk is absorbed.
4. Add the remaining milk, sugar, and vanilla extract.
5. Cook until the mixture thickens.
6. Serve warm or cold, garnished with cinnamon.

Baked Apples with Cinnamon (Kidney-Friendly Version)

Preparation Time: 50 minutes

Serves: 4

Calories: 120-170

Ingredients:

4 large apples, cored

2 tbsp honey

1/2 tsp ground cinnamon

1/4 cup raisins (optional)

1/4 cup chopped walnuts (optional, use if nuts are permissible in the diet)

Method of Preparation:

1. Preheat the oven to 350°F (175°C).
2. Place apples in a baking dish.
3. Mix honey and cinnamon, then spoon into the center of each apple.
4. Add raisins and walnuts if using.
5. Bake for 30-40 minutes until apples are tender.

SOUPS AND STEWS

Mushroom Cabbage Soup with Skinless Chicken

Preparation Time: 45 minutes

Serves: 4

Calories: 200

Ingredients:

200g skinless chicken breast, cubed

2 cups cabbage, shredded

1 cup mushrooms, sliced

1 medium onion, diced

2 cloves garlic, minced

4 cups low-sodium chicken broth

1 tbsp olive oil

Herbs (thyme, parsley) – as desired

Black pepper – to taste

Method of Preparation:

1. Heat olive oil in a large pot.
2. Add garlic and onion, sauté until translucent.
3. Add the chicken and cook until no longer pink.
4. Add mushrooms and cabbage, cook for a few minutes.
5. Pour in the low-sodium chicken broth, bring to a boil.
6. Reduce heat, add herbs and black pepper.
7. Simmer for 30 minutes.
8. Note: This recipe is low in sodium and potassium, suitable for kidney disease.

Zucchini and Bell Pepper Soup

Preparation Time: 30 minutes

Serves: 4

Calories: 150

Ingredients:

2 medium zucchinis, chopped

1 red bell pepper, chopped

1 onion, chopped

2 cloves garlic, minced

4 cups low-sodium vegetable broth

1 tbsp olive oil

Herbs (basil, oregano) – as desired

Black pepper – to taste

Method of Preparation:

1. In a pot, heat olive oil over medium heat.
2. Add garlic and onion, sauté.
3. Add zucchini and bell pepper, cook for 5 minutes.

4. Pour in the broth, add herbs and black pepper.

5. Bring to a boil, then simmer for 20 minutes.

6. Blend until smooth.

Vegetable Broth Soup

Preparation Time: 40 minutes

Serves: 4

Calories: 100

Ingredients:

4 cups low-sodium vegetable broth

1 cup carrots, diced

1 cup celery, diced

1 onion, diced

2 cloves garlic, minced

1 tbsp olive oil

Herbs (parsley, thyme) – as desired

Black pepper – to taste

Method of Preparation:

1. Heat olive oil in a pot.
2. Add garlic and onion, cook until soft.
3. Add carrots and celery, sauté for a few minutes.
4. Pour in the broth, add herbs and black pepper.
5. Bring to a boil, then simmer for 30 minutes.

Cabbage and Bell Pepper Stew

Preparation Time: 50 minutes

Serves: 4

Calories: 180

Ingredients:

2 cups cabbage, chopped

1 red bell pepper, chopped

1 onion, chopped

2 cloves garlic, minced

4 cups low-sodium vegetable broth

1 tbsp olive oil

Herbs (rosemary, thyme) – as desired

Black pepper – to taste

Method of Preparation:

1. In a pot, heat olive oil.
2. Add garlic and onion, cook until soft.
3. Add cabbage and bell pepper, sauté for 5 minutes.
4. Add the broth, herbs, and black pepper.
5. Bring to a boil, then simmer for 40 minutes.

Cauliflower Soup

Preparation Time: 35 minutes

Serves: 4

Calories: 120

Ingredients:

1 large cauliflower head, chopped

1 onion, chopped

2 cloves garlic, minced

4 cups low-sodium chicken or vegetable broth

1 tbsp olive oil

Herbs (sage, parsley) – as desired

Black pepper – to taste

Method of Preparation:

1. Heat olive oil in a pot. Sauté garlic and onion.
2. Add cauliflower, cook for 5 minutes.
3. Pour in the broth, add herbs and black pepper.
4. Bring to a boil, then simmer until cauliflower is soft.
5. Blend until smooth.

CONCLUSION

In conclusion, a well-managed diet is a cornerstone of treatment for you with stage 3 chronic kidney disease (CKD).

At this stage, the kidneys are moderately impaired, making it essential to adopt dietary practices that support kidney health while meeting the nutritional needs of older adults.

The primary goals are to minimize the progression of kidney damage, manage symptoms, and enhance overall quality of life.

Key aspects of a CKD stage 3 diet include moderating protein intake to reduce kidney strain, while ensuring sufficient high-quality protein to maintain muscle mass and overall health.

Sodium intake should be limited to control blood pressure and reduce the risk of fluid retention, which is paramount in preventing further kidney damage.

Potassium and phosphorus levels need careful monitoring and management, as imbalances can lead to significant health issues.

You should aim for a balanced diet rich in fruits, vegetables, whole grains, and lean proteins, providing necessary nutrients without overburdening the kidneys.

Fluid management is also critical, as too much or too little can exacerbate kidney problems and other health issues.

Caloric intake should be adequate to prevent malnutrition, a common concern in older adults, especially those with chronic illnesses.

Healthy fats should be included to support cardiovascular health, which is often compromised in CKD.

Regular consultations with healthcare professionals, including nephrologists and dietitians, are essential. They can provide personalized advice, taking into account the senior's overall health, nutritional needs, and specific CKD stage.

Finally, incorporating lifestyle modifications such as maintaining a healthy weight, engaging in regular physical activity, and avoiding smoking and excessive alcohol can further benefit kidney health.

Made in the USA
Middletown, DE
22 August 2024